Union League Club New York

Speeches Delivered at the Banquet Given to Honourable

Joseph H. Choate

Ambassador to England

Union League Club New York

Speeches Delivered at the Banquet Given to Honourable Joseph H. Choate
Ambassador to England

ISBN/EAN: 9783337425692

Printed in Europe, USA, Canada, Australia, Japan

Cover: Foto ©Thomas Meinert / pixelio.de

More available books at **www.hansebooks.com**

SPEECHES DELIVERED AT THE BANQUET GIVEN TO Hon. JOSEPH H. CHOATE, AMBASSA-DOR TO ENGLAND, AT THE UNION LEAGUE CLUB, NEW YORK, FRIDAY, FEBRUARY 17th, 1899. ✌ ✌ ✌ ✌ ✌ ✌ ✌ ✌ ✌ ✌ ✌

Mr. Elihu Root, President of the Club, Presided at the Banquet.

At the conclusion of the banquet, Mr. Root said:

GENTLEMEN : I ask you to join in drinking the health of the President of the United States.

The toast was drunk standing, and followed by three cheers for the President of the United States.

MR. ROOT : In view of the occasion which brings us together and all the sympathies that will go from this shore of the Atlantic to the other with our friend whom we meet to honor to-night, nothing can be so fitting as that now we join to the toast to the President of the United States, a toast to the health, long life and prosperous reign of the gracious lady to whom he will be accredited—Victoria, Queen of Great Britain and Ireland and Empress of India.

The toast was drunk standing, and followed by three cheers, and three cheers for Ambassador Choate.

MR. ROOT: Gentlemen of the Club and our guests : When Mr. Hay, the Ambassador from the United States to Great Britain, was recalled to take the office of Secretary of State and it became neces-sary to select a successor, there was every reason to be found in the rules governing the distribution of honor and emolument, for not selecting his succes-sor from the State of New York. A New Yorker, a former President of this Club, was discharging the difficult and delicate duties of Ambassador from the United States to the Republic of France. (Cheers.) Another New Yorker, an old and honored member of this Club, was discharging the equally difficult and delicate duties of Ambassador to the Empire of Germany. (Cheers.) Another New Yorker had but just received his passports and had ceased his residence as Minister to Spain. (Cheers.) And still another New Yorker had just been sent, for the second time, to be Minister to Turkey. (Cheers.) So that in accordance with all the rules that ordinarily govern such selections the remainder of this great country was entitled to consider that the last man to be selected as Ambassador to Great Britain to take the place of Mr. Hay should be a New Yorker. But there were conditions existing, there was a state of affairs patent to every intelligent man, which made it imperative that the President of the United States, in selecting a representative of the American people in the Court of England, should disregard all rules for the distribution of honor and of emolument and should go through the length and breadth of America to find the ablest and the best American (cheers), whatever his State, whatever his city, whatever his political claims might be; the ablest and the best we had to represent the American branch of the great Anglo-Saxon race at the birthplace of the race. (Cheers.) Yielding to the imperitive demands of the conditions that confronted him, the President came to this great city and selected our friend, not because he was a New Yorker, but in spite of his being a New Yorker, and because he was what we know him to be. (Applause.) This was not because of any of the ordinary requirements of diplomacy. It was not because there are any unsettled questions between England and America of extreme difficulty. There was no occasion for violating ordinary rules or taking especial pains in the selection of a representative because of boundary difficulties, or fishery questions, or sealing questions, or reciprocity questions. It was not because there was danger of conflict between England and America. It was not because England needed help from America or America needed help from England, but it was because the events of the last few months have revealed to the vision of the people of England and America a newly-found relation between those peoples, and between each of them and the great movement of mankind which is changing the face of civilization and making an epoch in history. (Applause). It was because swiftly coming events of the past year have revealed to our eyes, blind hitherto, the fact that during the past century, during our lifetime, a movement of civilized men has taken place more important in its character, more wide-spread in its effect, more potent in its influence upon civilization, than any that has occurred since the downfall of the Roman Empire. (Applause.) The movement is of that great race which we call Anglo-Saxon, though it is not—a composite race: Saxon and Norman and Dane, Gaul and Celt and Teuton—a race called Anglo-Saxon, but composite with all these elements of strength ; a race largely directed

in its impulses and its development by the initial
conditions of the Anglo-Saxon race and the promi-
nence of that element in its development; a race
moulded by the practice of freedom, having as the
cornerstone of its development individual liberty
and individual right, ordered and controlled by law;
a race which has imposed upon itself as a limitation
upon its own activity, its own passions and its own
impulses, the eternal principles of human justice;
(applause); a race whose character has been developed upon both sides of the Atlantic by the influences embodied in Magna Charta and the petition
of rights and the bill of rights and the habeas cor-
pus act and the American declaration and the
American Constitutions; a race which has grown
up in the practice of freedom and in obedience to
law, energized by the struggle of centuries with
nature, by adventure, by daring, by progress, by
strenuous effort; a race which has deep down,
ingrown, inherited in every member of its family
respect for human rights, for human justice, for
law, for order, for liberty. The majestic progress
of this new type of humanity, proceeding over the
entire face of the habitable globe, has been revealed
to us as one harmonious, united progress of all who
answer to the type, whether English or American.
(Applause.) Through that awakened vision we see
that the isolated instances in which we have gloried
are but part of a great whole. With Wolfe at
Quebec and Clive in India, with Jefferson buying
Louisiana and the Northwestern Territory, and

Seward buying Alaska; with the English trade following the flag and whitening every sea and American emigration swarming through the woods of Kentucky, Tennessee and Michigan and over the prairies and up the mountains and down the Pacific Slope; with Kitchener at Omdurman and Dewey at Manila (applause)—are seen but incidents of the same great story of the progress of the ideas of justice and liberty ; of the conception of human rights and the relations of man to man, which make the English and American type that we call Anglo-Saxon, the dominant type of the earth to-day. (Applause.) This does not mean that England and America are not to compete; that England and America are not to conflict; that they are not to seek each to gain advantage over the other. It does not mean that America is to enter upon a career of conquest, but it does mean this—recognition upon both sides of the Atlantic that the type is the same, and that where the type goes every individual that answers to the type is the gainer ; that whether it be along the St. Lawrence or the Mississippi, England gains ; whether it be along the Nile or the Ganges, America gains. That wherever the ideas that answer to our type of civilization, the ideas embodied in the great fundamental statutes of England and America ; the ideas protected by the great guarantees of individual liberty and individual opportunity that have made England and America great—wherever they go, whether it be under the meteor flag of England or the Stars and Stripes, every Englishman and every American is the gainer. (Applause.) And in the recognition of that great and basic fact of our history, the recognition of that great and controlling idea in the progress of civilization in our generation, and the generations to come, it was fitting that the representative of the President of the United States to the Queen of Great Britain should be more than that—that he should be a representative of the people of the United States to the people of Great Britain. (Applause). That through him the best thought and purpose of our people should be represented to the best mind and heart of the other branch of our race. (Applause.) And our friend may go upon this great mission with assured confidence that the people whom he represents are worthy of him. That they are brave a thousand battle fields and twice ten thousand heroic deeds of valor and fortitude on sea and land attest. But they are not only brave. They are just; they are law-abiding; they are magnanimous. A people's ideals point the way of the people's development, and the people's idols embody and illustrate their ideals, and it is a reassuring and a cheering thought that the men whom our countrymen hold closest to their hearts and highest in their hero-worship are great forgiving, patient, magnanimous men—Washington, Lincoln, and Grant. (Applause.) Let there be no fear in the heart of him who represents, for purposes of peace, a people trained in self-restraint by long years of obedience to law; a people who after the most terrible and bitter Civil War of history could present to mankind the unexampled spectacle that our country exhibits to-day, of North and South united in genuine fraternal feeling and emulation in the support of a common country; of the people of New York hailing the presence of Gen. Joseph Wheeler (applause.)—commanding American troops on the soil of New York, and the people of Atlanta lauding Major William McKinley to the skies as their chief magistrate. And he will be worthy of that great office. How well we know him. Others may tell of his learning and of the brilliant qualities that appeal to the multitude, but we know him as a man. He was but 41 years of age when we made him the President of this Club, and now, 67 years have left his eye bright and his locks brown, thank Heaven. And during all that time we have known him, his going out and his coming in day by day. We can speak to each other of those qualities that the great country knows little of. We know the purity of his character. We know that bright, happy, cheerful disposition that never fails to make the whole place brighter and all about him happier wherever he is. We know how active and broad his charity has been; his labors for education, for all good and benevolent causes in our community. We know how steadfast and enduring is his friendship; not perhaps the friendship of much clinking of glasses, of boisterous conviviality, but the deep and enduring friendship which answers to all drafts of a friend, always a present help in time of trouble and always steadfast and true. For my own part to the end of my life I shall deem it one of the happiest gifts of fortune that during many years of intimate association, sometimes allied and sometimes in conflict, I may be permitted after it all and through it all to call him friend. I know that we all feel that; that we all feel honored in his honor; that we all feel proud that our beloved country is to be represented in the most powerful Court of Europe by an American who measures up to the full stature of the greatest of Englishmen and who is our friend. (Applause).

And so we meet him here to bid him farewell and God speed, happy days, prosperous career, great achievements, fitting the achievements of his past, a happy home-coming to meet the friends and the hearty greetings that he will find when he comes. Join me in the health of the new Ambassador. (Prolonged cheers.)

SPEECH OF MR. CHOATE.

Mr. Root; gentlemen, friends of a lifetime: For the first time since I learned to speak the English language, which is henceforth to be the language of the world, I am at a loss for words (applause and laughter.) To receive such an honor as this from such men as these, who have seen me going to and fro and walking up and down in this city any time for the last forty years, is indeed the crowning honor of my life. And when I look around these tables and see the men whom I have labored with in almost every cause to which this Club has been devoted since its organization; when I see them headed by such old heroes as Charles L. Tiffany and LeGrand B. Cannon—(applause)—I confess that I am absolutely overwhelmed by the honor that you have sought to do me. (Applause.)

You will not expect me, harassed and overcome by the thousand duties that press upon me in these few last days before my departure to have prepared anything like a formal farewell address that might, perhaps, be more fitting to an occasion like this; and so I am sure that you will indulge me if for this once I rely almost entirely upon spontaneous combustion. (Laughter.) But how could I fail to respond with all my heart to such a splendid demonstration of friendship and good will as is presented here to-night? Here have I been engaged in the activities of life for so many decades, too often in vigorous and earnest combat, and yet I find here to-night my oldest friends and my dearest foes uniting to bid me a God speed and safe return. There are no friends like the old friends; there are no faces like the old faces, and I assure you if I had known how hard it was to sever the ties that bind me to New York and to America, I should really have insisted upon spending the remainder of my days at home. I hope—I expect to make many new friends, many worthy and valuable friends upon the other side of the water, but how can they for one moment make good the place of these? No, gentlemen; all the honors of life, all its prizes, all its treasures, all its rewards are not, in my judgment, to be compared with the good will and the good opinion of the men who have known me and walked side by side with me all my life. (Applause.) And then that such an event as this, in my honor, should take place in this building! That this Club, with which so many of the happiest and noblest hours of my life have been identified should furnish forth a host of friends like these! What memories the very name of this association calls up! What a school it has been for an Ambassador who shall represent the real America in any country of the world! (Applause.) A school of unconditional loyalty from the beginning. A school of earnest patriotism. A school for the elevation of all that is good and great in the social and political life of America. (Good. Good.) My mind goes back to a very early day in the history of this Club, and many of these who are seated at these tables go back with me to recall what noble causes have here been espoused; what great things have been attempted at least, that should make America greater and better than it was before. I recall the struggle in which it took such an earnest part when the first shot at Fort Sumter aroused the indignation of the North to the defense of the beleaguered capitol at Washington and the imperiled existence of the country itself. How earnest they were! How devoted and untiring in the support of the Government from the beginning to the end of that great cause! I recollect what they have done from first to last since 1863 throughout this Club's existence, for the elevation of the public service and the public morals. How Civil Service Reform, of which the most illustrious advocate sits here on my right [Governor Roosevelt], found here its advocates and supporters. How the cause of sound money has never once appealed to it in vain. (Applause.) How, when the flag of the country was in danger, a rally to its support always found a centre here. And so I flatter myself that having been trained here and shared in your labors and your efforts for the public good, I have had a thorough schooling as a real American, and to say no more of myself I will make you just one promise, that I will return at the end of my sojourn as good an American as I go away. (Prolonged applause.)

Now I am not willing to appropriate to myself much, if any, of my brother Root's most flattering words. That they should flow from his lips—the lips of a friend who has been very dear to me for a quarter of a century—is most encouraging ; but I know perfectly well that a life spent in forensic struggle is a wholly inadequate preparation for diplomatic service. (Laughter.) I shall have to rely on some other qualities than those which I have developed in the practice of the law if I am to succeed in this new employment. (Laughter.) I shall rely upon a happy temperament, worth millions to any man (laughter and applause) ; on unfailing good nature, which no discussion can ruffle (laughter) ; upon honest intentions ; upon plain dealing and true speaking, conscious all the time of the great dignity and the rare interests of the country that I represent ; paying just regard always to those of that great country to which I am accredited, and then, if I fail, it will not be because I have any doubt of the encouragement and the good will and support of you and of all my countrymen. (Prolonged applause.)

I believe that never before since the people of the United States ordained our great Constitution to form a more perfect union, to establish justice, to provide for the common defense, to promote the general welfare and to secure the blessings of liberty to themselves and their children, did they send any representative abroad who had greater cause to be proud of his own country, or who was sure to receive a more hearty and cordial welcome and greeting for its sake from the country to which he is sent, than now (applause); and that will be a welcome not merely from the English Government but also from the English people. I believe, from all that I have ever read or heard, that the English people have never at any time been in the least hostile to the people of America. (Applause.) God has made of one blood these two mighty nations. Their common origin, common language and common literature, the English Bible, and the Common Law have bound their hearts together in a union which no rivalry of interests, no exigencies of politics, no blunders of government on either side, have ever permanently impaired. (Applause.)

And one thing more I want to say, which I believe from the bottom of my heart to be an absolute truth, and that is that in that august and venerable woman who, after more than sixty years of sovereignty, still reigns supreme in the hearts of her people, America, from the beginning, has found a steadfast and a faithful friend. (Applause.)

Now, it is true, as my brother Root has intimated, that this fast and earnest friendship which has found and is finding every day such abundant expression on both sides of the Atlantic, is not going to change the course of human events or of human nature. It will not make water run up hill after all. We shall still have our rival interests. It cannot but be that the rivalry will be intense, and sometimes possibly bitter; but this we do believe, by reason of this well-spring of friendship which has grown up so steadfastly of late, that we shall contend as friendly rivals, and that all our differences hereafter will be settled by peaceful negotiation and friendly arbitration, and never once again by any resort to arms. (Applause.)

Now there is one interest of the United States of America which, in my judgment, is paramount to any other and all others combined, and that interest is the preservation of peace. (Cries of "Good! Good!") I mean not peace at any price, but peace always when it can be preserved with honor. (Cries of "Good! Good!") Not peace with one nation only, but with all the nations, great and small, of all the earth. (Applause.) And after all, with this dear mother country of ours—or, as I prefer to call her and regard her, this elder sister of ours—our friendship should only be a little more close and a little more binding than that which has existed, and still exists, between us and other great nations. (Cries of "Good! Good!") Can America ever forget, for instance, how steadfast, how unfailing, has been the friendship which Russia has shown and manifested for this country (applause) for more than a century now? Can we ever forget that undying debt of gratitude and obligation which we owe to our sister republic of France? (Cries of "Good! Good!") France, without whose aid this infant republic, at least in that century, could hardly have come to be an independent nation. (Applause). Can anything tear out from the veins of that composite creature, the modern and typical American who occupies the great basin between the Alleghanies and the Rocky Mountains and who rules and controls this country and this continent; can anything tear out from his veins that Teutonic strain which binds us to Germany and makes us, as a people, so near of kin to that mighty nation ? (Applause). And, yet, for all that, we mean to cultivate by all means in our power this friendship, this tie of brotherhood and fraternity, and of common family that exists between us and England. And with what hope? Why, as our rival interests shall be settled between us, peacefully, amicably, honorably, so when the identity and unity of our interests leads our two nations to work together, our common action shall always tend to promote and fortify peace, justice, liberty and civilization all the world around. (Applause.)

And now, why should an American feel prouder of his country to-day than he ever felt before? For I like to carry that as my greatest and sweetest possession in my heart as I cross the water. (Applause.) There are men still living and within the sound of my voice, men whose personal recollection and personal action—there are several of them sitting before me—go back and form a part of the history of the country for a full half-century. And what has not America achieved within that period, brief in the life of any nation? I do not suppose that ever yet in all history there was such progress made by any people as ours have made in that brief space of time. There are men sitting here who have taken part in that great material development by which a little score of States upon the Atlantic coast, hardly extending half-way to the Mississippi, have in that short period, filled and conquered the continent and made the world listen to the busy hum of industry in the homes of seventy millions of people. There never was, I believe, such progress made before in any time or in any clime. And then such gigantic strides as we have made, often apparently the result of wars which were deprecated, dreaded, opposed with the most honest motive by the most patriotic citizens of the country. Some of these gentlemen remember, as I am old enough to remember, the outbreak of the Mexican War. I sat at the feet of Gamaliel and learned how much to be regretted it was, but it came. By the will of the people it was fought, and by the Providence that reigned over this country, it resulted, as you all know, in the immense development, the immense aggrandizement and enrichment of the whole country. The admission of California, all the wealth and new energy and enterprise that followed upon that were great and invaluable blessings to this country. And then the Civil War, which seemed at the outset to be absolutely destructive for the time being of all prosperity, and almost of the hope of our national existence, resulted in the creation of a new America, with new enterprise, new energy, new life, bringing the redemption not only of the South but of the North and the inspiration of a mighty people who had not realized their strength before. And then in this last twelve months what has not been achieved? I will not enter upon any eulogy upon any person, upon any official, civil or military, but I call to your attention the great things that have been accomplished in this short period of time. In the first place the restoration of universal prosperity throughout the length and breadth of the land. (Applause.) This banquet could almost be accepted as an illustration of the prosperity that now smiles upon our people. (Laughter). The public credit, which only three or four years ago was wavering, has been established and seems now to command the confidence not only of our own people, but of every other people in the world. (Applause.) And then, too, a great work of humanity has been accomplished in the extinction over every foot of American soil of the last vestige of Spanish power and Spanish oppression—(applause)—brought to a culmination only the last few days by the ratification of the Treaty of Peace which one of the Commissioners now present had such a great hand in framing. (Applause.) But more than all this the people of the United States have become united as they have never been united before, in support of the institutions, the glory and the interests of their common country. And still better than that, to go back to the very point at which I began, the achievements of our army and our navy have developed a prowess and a vigor that has not only commanded the respect but the apprehension of other nations—(applause)—and I believe it to be absolutely true that at this moment our country is on better terms with every other nation in the world than she has ever been before. (Applause.) And best of all, the fruit of this war that has come so speedily and so happily to an end, is the restoration of that absolute confidence and abiding good will which exists, and I believe always has existed, but now flames forth more strongly than ever before, between us and all the English speaking peoples of the Globe. (Applause.)

Now, gentlemen, perhaps I have expressed my sentiments quite as fully and freely as my official restrictions permit. I know how soon I shall be absolutely tongue-tied, and so let me say that to-night I speak for myself alone, but I want before I take my seat again to thank you for this most cordial greeting, this most affectionate farewell with which you have honored me to-night. How shall I reciprocate it? Will you not all, each, individually and collectively, visit me at my new home? I assure you that the latch string will be always out. I may not have extra plates enough every day to entertain you all, but in the course of the few years of my pilgrimage I shall hope to receive each of you under my roof. (Prolonged applause.)

The President called for three cheers for Ambassador Choate, which were given.

Mr. Root: Gentlemen: I give you the health, the prosperity of the administration which sends Mr. Choate as Ambassador to England, and with that toast I couple the name of the Attorney-General of the United States. (Applause.)

SPEECH OF ATT'Y-GEN'L GRIGGS.

Mr. President, and fellow-members of the Union League Club: I came here desiring to be dis-associated from my official relations in order that I might join with you, my brethren, in congratulating our honored guest upon the distinguished service to which he is to be sent and in wishing him God speed. I desired to come also as a member of the profession to which he belongs, whose members as you all know, however belligerent they may appear in the forensic field, and however savagely they may attack each other, can always walk together arm in arm from the court room and provoke the suspicions of their clients as to their true allegiance—(laughter)—a profession of whose members it has been said, "They work hard, they live well and they die poor." This particular member, as you know, has in his profession worked hard, and since he has dined with the Union League Club you know he has lived well, and if we all go to the Court of St. James and visit him, as he has invited us to do, considering the amount of salary the United States pays, he will probably die poor. (Laughter and applause.) He goes to one of the oldest established civilized governments upon the face of the earth ; a government that was old before we began to be ; which had spent millions on millions of dollars in building up and improving itself and its institutions before we began to provide the necessaries of life for our own national household. Until recently the United States has had all she could do to take care of herself. In the early days it was a struggle to stand firmly on her feet. Consider the contrast between the day when John Adams went, the first accredited Minister of the New Republic to his former sovereign, King George, and to-day, when this honored member of this Club goes from this nation of seventy million people to our great, friendly sister nation across the water. When sturdy John Adams met the King and addressed him, in his introduction he said to him that he desired above all things to bring about a restoration of the kindly sentiments that should prevail between two such peoples ; a restoration in a word of the old good humor that should prevail between peoples that had the same language, the same religion and kindred blood. Many years passed before that generous wish was fulfilled, but to-day it has been fulfilled and that same good humor that he desired and labored and prayed for does prevail between these peoples. (Applause.)

When somebody asked Lord Wellington what were the peculiar characteristics of the soldiers that composed his army on the Peninsula he said, "Well, the English are most interested when there is a plentiful supply of beef, and the Irish are the happiest when we are in a country where the vine grows, and the Scotch are the most delighted when the paymaster comes." Now, our friend goes from a country whose citizens and whose soldiers recognize and rejoice in all three of these characteristics. (Laughter.) It is a greater country than it was even when our last Ambassador was accredited to the Court of St. James. Some one asked a man whom he met with his dinner pail, if he worked hard, and he said he did and the hours were too long. "Why," said he, "sometimes I work so long that when I go home at night I meet myself going to work in the morning"; and so now our friend goes as the representative of a country—Uncle Sam's country—as to which it may be said that when Uncle Sam is starting out, by way of the Suez Canal, for his Pacific possessions, he may meet himself coming back the other way. (Laughter and applause.)

But, my friends, it is not only as Mr. Choate said, with Great Britain that we are friends and at peace and good will, but we aim to be at peace and at good will with all mankind. The United States is not, and it never has been, a nation that desired to become the aggressor upon or the oppressor of any people. (Applause.) They have possessed the spirit of liberators, not the spirit of oppressors. They have not boasted that they have subdued mankind, but rather that they have raised mankind up. If there is any characteristic of this people that distinguishes it, it is its generosity, its benevolence, its good will. What people in suffering or distress has not experienced the generosity of the American citizen, the American merchant and the American individual in contributions for their relief? Has it been the yellow fever sufferer? Has it been the famine stricken friends of ours in the Green Isle? Has it been the murdered Christians of

Armenia? Has there been any people on the face of the earth where the hand of the oppressor has been hard, or where misery and misfortune have come, that the substantial sympathy of America has not gone in generous relief? (Applause.) And so, my friends, the generous people of this country believe that now, in these days, and under these circumstances, they are going forward, not to oppress, not to destroy, but to relieve, to strengthen and to build up. (Cries of "Good! Good!") They have no desire for an expansion of territory that shall be unprincipled, or purely selfish. If any one thinks that the American people are not actuated by the highest aims, he can get no support for that doctrine from any nation on the face of the earth. Those who say it must be men of our nation and of our own people. That which we have done, that which we have taken, we have done and taken with the consent, with the substantial approval of the nations of the earth, not one of whom has dared to challenge our right. (Applause.) What has been done has been done; whether it has been irresistible destiny or whatever it has been, it is accomplished, and what, in the face of that, is the duty of loyal Americans? You remember the old toast of the old American Commodore: "Our country; may she always be right, but right or wrong, our country"! (Applause.) But I know of a finer and nobler expression of that sentiment that is appropriate today. It was uttered by that great lawyer, that great orator, that great statesman, who was the kinsman of our honored guest to-night. It was uttered forty years ago when he was speaking of that great American statesman and expounder of the Constitution, Daniel Webster, and of him, Rufus Choate said: "He did not favor a premature and unprincipled extension of territory, but he saw, and he rejoiced to see, if America continued just, and continued brave, and the Union lasted, how widely— to what tropic and pacific seas—she must spread; but when the annexation was made, when the line was drawn, when the treaty was signed, then he went for her however butted and bounded. Then he stood steadfast by the compact of annexation and there was no line so remote, no spot so distant, that he would not plant upon it the ensign all-radiant, that no foreign aggression might come." This was, said he, "The very Websterianism of Webster," and that should be to-day the very Americanism of Americans. (Applause.) Who has doubt of the ability of this nation to deal with any problem that it may undertake when it can call to its service from the ranks of this Club a gentleman so able, so distinguished, so capable as our friend, who has attained the age of 67 years without having hitherto given his country the benefit of his official service? Does it not illustrate that we have tens of thousands of men of ability in this country that we can call upon if we want? Who are those that are managing the finances, the businesses, the railroads, the factories of this country, except the very foremost men of ability and of administration? (Applause.) We do not mean, we Americans, that these questions shall be submitted merely to those who desire personal advantage from them, but I am proud to believe—and I consider it an insult to America for anybody to assert the contrary—that her people desire to have the best ability, the most patriotic service, that kind of service which they can obtain in their own great enterprises, brought to bear upon these new problems, that out of them may work not only new glory for our country, but new prosperity for ourselves and for all those peoples whom we shall reach. (Applause.)

My friends, I am not fearful of the old ship of State. She is sailing steadily on as she has ever sailed. She has a good sound hull beneath her; she has triple expansion engines; she has a crew of American blood that are generous, benevolent, kindly, but whose aim is very deadly! (Cries of "Good! Good!") We do not desire to humiliate those that oppose us. We only desire that they shall cease to oppose. We have not sought the sword of our conquered enemy. Grant refused to take Lee's, and Bob Evans to take Cervera's. And on this ship of State there is a pilot; clear-eyed, looking forward only for the beacon lights of truth, steadfast of purpose, with a brave heart, a courageous soul, and a hopeful spirit. Some of the passengers I admit, the vessel having reached rough waters, are a little seasick; they do not want to finish the voyage; they want the vessel to put about and turn back to harbor and moor up to the wharf ; but, my friends, you know that the fears and perturbations of a seasick soul, lest the ship shall sink, never made any sensible captain turn back to port. (Laughter and applause.)

And so I bid our new Ambassador God speed. He goes as the representative of a greater country than any Ambassador ever carried the credentials of to the Court of St. James before. (Applause.) Some centuries ago that magnificent old Englishman, Sir Francis Drake, while he lay in hiding on the Isthmus of Panama waiting for the tinkle of the mule bell that should reveal to him the coming of the Spanish treasure train, climbed a tree—a tall tree—from which he looked out, and beyond him saw the mysterious expanse of the Pacific, and his heart was fired with the desire to sail there and attach for his King the land that he knew must lie beyond ; and he descended and knelt at the foot of the tree—this reverent old pirate (laughter)—and he promised the Almighty that he would ever serve Him if he might be allowed to live long enough to sail into that mysterious sea, across those expansive stretches of water where Drake saw and still lie the new possessions of America. But no longer do we need the slow white wings of the old English frigates to get there ; to-day the Congress of the United States is considering a proposition to unite those distant islands with this continent by the nerves of the electric cable. Consider the difference, my friends, and remember then that as we stand now at the utmost verge of the 19th century, America says to the world and to all the people of the world, we are trying, striving, working to advance the welfare of the human race. We invite the co-operation, we will gladly join in co-operation as one nation may with others, in this grand work. For selfish aggrandizement, nothing, but for humanity, for civilization, everything. (Applause.)

Mr. ROOT: Gentlemen; I am going to give you a toast to the people of the country to which Mr. Choate is accredited, and to ask to respond to that toast a native of that country who is as good an American as ever trod the soil on this side of the Atlantic. To the people of Great Britain. And with that I couple the name of the Hon. William Bourke Cockran. (Applause and three cheers for Bourke Cockran.)

SPEECH OF MR. COCKRAN.

Gentlemen of the Union League Club, I am deeply indebted to your historic organization for the hospitality which has enabled me to join in this banquet, than which a higher compliment has seldom been offered to a citizen. Its cordiality, the characters of the men participating in it, the warm affection displayed for the guest of honor, all combine to make it a tribute so impressive that, of itself, it would be a substantial crown to a successful career. (Applause.)

I think we all may find in Mr. Choate's appointment a two-fold source of congratulation. It tends to refute the statement so often made that our domestic politics are hopelessly corrupt, while it affords every reason to believe that our international consequence will be sustained and promoted.

It would be useless to deny that many good citizens have come to regard political organizations as mere engines of corruption. If this be true, the end of the Republic is in sight. If both our political parties, embracing as they do a vast majority of our citizens, be hopelessly sunk in servility, corruption, and degradation, the government which rests upon them must itself be so corrupt as to render it a menace to property, and a government which restricts industry by endangering its fruits has already entered upon the pathway to destruction.

The selection of Mr. Choate for one of the most conspicuous places in the public service is a striking proof that our political conditions are neither abject nor desperate. A stream cannot rise higher than its source. Good cannot flow from evil. An appointment made with the active support of a party organization could scarcely be of such a character as to command the approval of the patriotic and the intelligent if that organization itself were a fountain of corruption. (Applause.)

Do not, my friends, believe for a moment that I am eulogizing the management of our parties. To recognize the hopeful features of any condition is not to condone, tolerate, or approve its objectionable features, but rather to measure the resources available for its improvement. The citizen who prefers to labor for the amelioration of our politics rather than waste his energies in deploring their shortcomings must find a source of encouragement in the fact that a party manager—a boss—call him what you will—has been able to support for high public office the conspicuous exemplar of professional ability and civic virtue without endangering or weakening his leadership.

While Mr. Choate's appointment should be especially cheering to those whose gloomy views of our politics have led them to despair of the republic, it must be a source of profound satisfaction to citizens of every party and condition, for all of them believe that his duties will be discharged with credit to himself, honor to his government and advantage to the people of both countries.

Of course, a discussion of Mr. Choate's embassy would disappoint the expectations of his audience if it omitted reference to its most important aspect. Whatever may be its immediate effect on himself, we all hope and believe that its permanent fruit will be an improvement in the relations between the people of Great Britain and this country. (Applause.) In this respect, I believe his appointment is the very best that could have been made. (Applause.) If any proof were needed that Mr. Choate's mission will be an effective force to promote the co-operation of both countries in every laudable purpose for which nations can unite with profit, he himself has furnished it in his admirable speech this evening. (Applause,)

Like my friend, Mr. Root, who has discussed this mission with the eloquence of a statesman and the warmth of a friend, I prefer to regard Mr. Choate as a representative from one branch of the Anglo-Saxon race to another, rather than to interpret his commission according to the technical language accrediting him to a Court or to a Government. What is this race to which, as he says, we persist in believing Mr. Choate's mission is really directed, no matter what may be the language of his formal credentials? Mr. Root tells us that the word Anglo-Saxon is a misnomer, because it is applied to a race composed of the English, the Celt and the American. I do not believe that the word is a misnomer so far as it is descriptive of the English people, while I think it is utterly misleading when applied to the English Government. The race whose valor in war and genius in peace have reflected on

England a glory which encircles the world is not the race which dominates the Government of England. The English people are Anglo-Saxon; the English governing class is Norman. I do not believe we can understand England's position in the world unless we realize as Mr. Choate must realize, from his familiarity with English jurisprudence, that the Norman, while he has disappeared from every other country through which he passed fighting, pillaging, conquering, still maintains his identity in England. And as the Anglo-Norman has preserved all his racial characteristics, so also has the Anglo-Saxon. The Norman has never relinquished his hold on the throne established on the field of Hastings; the Anglo-Saxon has never ceased to defend that ancient common law which has been through all ages the impregnable rampart of freedom. To this day the Norman is as adventurous and as masterful as ever he was, while the Anglo-Saxon is still as industrious and devoted to liberty as he was in the days of the good King Edward.

The whole history of England for eight centuries is a history of the struggle between the English people to maintain Anglo-Saxon law and Anglo-Saxon liberty against the oppressive institutions of feudalism fastened upon them for a while by successful foreign invasion. The irrepressible hostility between these races has been fought out on English soil, and there the spirit of Anglo-Saxon liberty has triumphed over the Norman spirit of personal dominion.

The Norman has always shown himself an effective force for foreign conquest, while the Anglo-Saxon, slower to take up arms, has proved himself the better soldier when the field of contest was his own soil, and the stake of battle the liberties of his country. (Applause.)

The Norman, compelled to respect liberty and tolerate freedom within the limits of England, has yet been able to embark the English people in schemes to establish beyond the sea institutions of government which would not be tolerated upon English soil. This explains what to many is incomprehensible—the fact that English rule bears such widely different fruits in different places—in some quarters proving itself salutary, beneficent, popular, and in others oppressive, sanguinary, and execrated.

The Norman has never crossed the sea except to engage in schemes of military adventure ; the Anglo-Saxon never leaves his native land except to establish a home where he will cultivate the fields and raise a family in the fear of God and the love of liberty. (Applause.)

Wherever we find England engaged in schemes of conquest, pillage or violence, there the Norman spirit of adventure is active. Wherever we find self-governing, self-respecting communities speaking the English tongue, maintaining the English law, there we find the Anglo-Saxon spirit of justice bearing fruits of freedom, morality and progress. (Applause.)

English history may be described as a compromise between the opposing influences of the Norman and the Anglo-Saxon upon the destinies of England. The things which have made England glorious and respected are the fruits of Anglo-Saxon influence, the policies which have made her hated, feared, and distrusted are the products of Norman violence and aggression.

Wherever English authority is exercised to maintain the English law, there the authority of the English crown rests, not on force, but on affection—there the English flag is cherished by loyal hearts which would freely bleed in defense of it. Wherever England's military power has been used to establish a government not intended to maintain English law, but to violate it, there her moral weight has been discredited, there her authority is maintained solely by arms, sometimes against resistance, always in the teeth of an ever-deepening and and ever-darkening hatred.

The Norman has contributed some pages to history which Englishmen read with pride, but the whole world is enriched by the enduring contributions of the Anglo-Saxon to the progress of civilization. Crecy, Poictiers, Agincourt, the victories in the Low Countries, were the fruits of Norman valor. The literature of Shakespeare, the philosophy of Bacon, the law of Coke, of Hale and of Blackstone—that law which is at once the pride and the hope of the human race, the light of progress, the shield of liberty, the rampart of order, the fountain of our own constitutional system, the vital principle of free institutions everywhere—are the fruits of Anglo-Saxon virtue and of Anglo-Saxon genius.

History does not record an instance of violence by the Anglo-Saxon except where he was persuaded that it was necessary to draw the sword for the defense of justice or the vindication of liberty. To rouse the Norman to warlike activity it was never necessary to persuade him of anything except that there was a good prospect for a fight. (Laughter.)

It is often said that among the masses of the American people there has been a rooted dislike of England. I believe this to be a misconception. The English masses have never given us cause of dislike and we have never cherished any hostility to them. The English classes have often shown themselves distrustful of us, and we have returned the feeling. The oppressive measures which provoked the American Revolution did not proceed from the English people, but from the English court and the English throne. The American Republic is itself the triumphant fruit of Anglo-Saxon jurisprudence. Our Revolution was not an uprising against the English jurisprudence, but a movement in defense of it. It did not overturn the English law in America, but it drove out of this country the English officials who had attempted to overturn it. The first fruit of our Revolution was to make that ancient common law the birthright of every American citizen. The first amendment of our Constitution was the adoption, word for word, of the Bill of

Rights—that Bill of Rights established by the English yeomen and the English commoner against the fierce resistance of the Norman cavalier and Norman court—that Bill of Rights which marked the triumph of liberty in England at the close of the 17th Century, after a struggle of six hundred years—established forever on this side of the Atlantic at the close of the 18th century.

Between two countries, united by the ties of a common tongue and a common jurisprudenee, an alliance is natural and advisable. Now, what must be the basis of such an alliance? Between two such nations there is but one basis possible, and that is justice. Not all the treaties in the world, whatever their provisions, could enlist this people in schemes of aggression and conquest ; no treaty is necessary to insure their co-operation in any undertaking which makes for the uplifting of the human race by the spread of that jurisprudence which has shown itself the most effective means of establishing justice.

Mr. Choate has said to-night with great truth that rivalries between the two countries are inevitable. Such rivalries, indeed, must exist, but they will be rivalries of commerce, rivalries to promote the progress of civilization and the improvement of the human race. Pray God these two countries shall never again draw the sword against each other or against any other people to further schemes of conquest or oppression. (Applause.)

We need no treaty to enlist the people of this country in support of the jurisprudence which is the vital principle of this republic. Mr. Choate will not have spent many days in England before he will realize that there is a keener appreciation in this country of the things that constitute England's real glory than he will find in London. Nowhere, indeed, are the sources of England's greatness less understood than in the English court and the London drawing-rooms.

The Queen's Jubilee, two years ago, was one of the greatest pageants that ever occurred in the English metropolis. It was a festival graced by the presence of the distinguished gentleman sitting here upon my right [Mr. Whitelaw Reid], as Special Ambassador of the United States. Yet that pageant embraced no representatives of those English institutions which everywhere receive the sincere compliment of imitation. It comprised representatives of every element that constituted the empire's military strength. There were soldiers resplendent in uniforms of every color. In the ranks were armed men whose skins were of different hues. Every quarter of the globe contributed to its splendor some display of naval or military power, but from one end of that procession to the other there was not an author to represent the stately literature which forms the chief intellectual treasure of the human race; not a judge to represent the jurisprudence which is the shield of English liberty; not a member of either House of Parliament to represent the constitutional system which is England's security and her safety. England's greatness does not rest upon her arms or upon possessions. Her strength and her glory are her system of representative government and her ancient common law. No country cares to model its military establishment on that of England. Every country which is striving to reach prosperity through the protection of free institutions seeks to make its civil government conform to England's constitutional system. The Ambassador to whom we wish God speed to-night, himself the ornament and exponent of that common law which, transplanted to this soil, has here achieved its most stately growth, by every word that may fall from his lips, by the whole lesson of his life and character, will promote and encourage love, respect, and appreciation for the civilizing influences of Anglo-Saxon jurisprudence and Anglo-Saxon freedom. (Applause.)

Thus will he encourage an alliance between these two countries that will be enduring, because it will be beneficial ; an alliance that will not be for the selfish interests of the classes, but for the common interests of the masses ; an alliance not resting upon the intrigues of the drawing-rooms, but on the consciences of all the people on both sides of the Atlantic ; an alliance, not for territorial aggrandizement, or the suppression of freedom in any quarter of the globe, but an alliance for the spread of that jurisprudence which everywhere makes for order, progress and liberty ;—an alliance that will promote the establishment of God's Kingdom on earth by the diffusion of God's justice throughout the world. (Loud applause.)

Mr. ROOT: Gentlemen, I give you the profession upon which our friend is about to enter, and I couple with this toast the name of an honored member of this Club who has had a most distinguished career in the forefront of American diplomacy, as Ambassador of the United States to the Republic of France, as special Ambassador of the United States upon the occasion of the Queen's Jubilee in England, and as a member of the Peace Commission which negotiated the treaty with Spain, just ratified by the American Senate—the Hon. Whitelaw Reid. (Applause.)

SPEECH OF MR. REID.

Mr. President, I am not here to make a speech. If I were, I should remain silent before the Governor of my State; I should remain silent before this older and better soldier [turning to Gov. Morton at his side] in the field to which you assign me; I should remain silent before all these gentlemen whom I see ranged along the platform, eager to speak. I ran away from another engagement, simply to join in your congratulations and good wishes —nothing more. But entering this room and witnessing this extraordinary demonstration, I am reminded of some small experiences and personal reminiscences which to me are very agreeable. When I was first asked, many years ago, to undertake public service abroad, the offer came to me primarily from an eminent statesman, with whom the name and the work of your guest have been indissolubly associated through his whole professional life. When, some years later, I was able to accept another such offer, the first almost of those who were good enough to organize a small dinner here for me, by way of launching me safely out of the country, was your guest to-night. And to prove that he had no more ill-will in launching me out of the country than we manifest towards him now when we speed his parting, he was equally prompt in aiding to organize another dinner to welcome me back. It seems to be my turn now.

He is going to a city which will thoroughly appreciate him and thoroughly enjoy him; and to a city which likewise he will thoroughly appreciate and enjoy. He is going to the real capital, if there is one, of the race to which we all belong—the race which girdles, and civilizes, and leads, if it does not rule, the world. He will enjoy it ; but we shall enjoy it more. We shall be very proud of our Ambassador there ; proud of him as a representative New Yorker, and prouder still as a worthy representative of a continental republic. (Applause.)

He will not find his bed all roses, nor his days all holidays. He will discover before long, if I am not greatly mistaken, or if his experience does not differ widely from that of those who have gone before him, that an Ambassador at that post who conscientiously discharges all his varied duties, and, above all, strives to satisfy the varied wishes of the great American people, is simply the hardest-worked and worst-paid servant in that whole big city. And yet there are people who like it ! He will like it. He will fill the place on all its sides and will adorn it. I congratulate you on the Ambassador you are sending out, and congratulate equally the country that sends him and the country to which he is sent. I predict for him a brilliant career and a most useful one, and I heartily wish it for him ; and I join with you all—and with this I shall close, since I ought not to speak at all in advance of these others—I join most heartily in your good-byes and God speed. (Applause.)

Mr. ROOT: Now, gentlemen, the concluding toast of the evening will be fittingly the toast that comes home to our own State—the State of New York—·of our Ambassador's home and our home, and with that I couple the name, the unknown name of Theodore Roosevelt. (Cheers and applause.)

SPEECH OF GOV. ROOSEVELT.

Mr. President and gentlemen : When our host spoke with such just eulogy of the Anglo-Saxon race, I could not help turning to Mr. Cockran and asking him on our joint behalf where the Dutch and Irish come in. I think that our presence here to-night emphasizes just what he meant, that those who belong to the English-speaking race by adoption, by spirit, by the inheritance of common ideas and common aspirations, have the right to hail the renewed friendship between the English-speaking people of the British Isles and the English-speaking people of this great continent exactly as have any of those whose forefathers came over in the "Mayflower" or first settled on the banks of the James ; and when our Ambassador goes to England I know he will remember not only the facts that have been put before you in the magnificent oratory of Mr. Cockran to-night, but one other fact, something that supplements what Mr. Cockran said. Mr. Cockran did well to dwell upon the place that has been won by the great qualities of the English-speaking peoples ; he did well to dwell upon how much we have owed to the feats of the great captains of industry, to the feats of the men of letters, of the men of law. But the Ambassador will also remember how much has been owing to the men who carried the sword. I see here in the audience before me many men who either wear, or could if they chose wear, the button that shows that they fought in the most righteous war of modern times; and the statesmanship of Abraham Lincoln would have come to naught had it not been for the soldiership of Grant, Sherman and Sheridan, of Thomas and of Farragut. (Applause.)

There have been other races as great in war as the English-speaking people, but they have not been as great in peace. There have been other races as great in peace but they have not shown themselves as great in war. The great point in the up-building of the so-called Anglo-Saxon people (I am unable to go into the nice ethnic distinction that would make of Clive, of Wellington, and Nelson, Normans —I much doubt whether Washington, and Andrew Jackson, and Grant, and Phil Sheridan, were Normans), but the great point in the up-building of the English-speaking peoples, in the up-building of our own nation has been that, together with the love for peace has gone the ability to carry on war; that with the love for letters, with the love of orderly obedience to law, has gone the capacity to stand up stoutly for the right when menaced by any foreign foe. (Applause.) And the Ambassador will go to England holding his head the higher, not only because he goes from a land that has won such triumphs of peace; not only because he goes from a land that has added to the reputation of the jurist of the world because it has produced men like himself; that has added to the oratory of the world by the presence in it of men like yourself, Mr. Cockran, but he will go holding his head the higher because Dewey's guns thundered at Manila and the Spanish ships were sunk off Santiago Bay. (Applause.) All honor to the men of peace ; and all honor also to the race that has shown that besides men of peace it can in time of need bring forth men who are mighty in battle. (Applause.)

I feel that this Club has a peculiar right to pride itself upon sending Mr. Choate as Ambassador, because Mr. Choate stands as the architype of the kind of American citizenship which this club prides itself upon having produced. The greatest master of the English language that the world has ever seen ; the writer with the keenest insight into human nature that any writer has had since the days of Holy Writ, has stated to mankind as his advice, "Above all to thine own self be true Thou can'st not then be false to any man." Mr. Choate has stated that he will come back as he goes, a good American, and we do not need the assurance, for he could come back nothing else. (Applause.) The first requisite in the statesmanship that shall benefit mankind, so far as we are concerned, is that that statesmanship shall be thoroughly American. No American statesman who forgot to be first and foremost an American was ever yet able to do anything to benefit the world as a whole. The world moves upward as a whole by means of the people who make the different countries of the world move upward ; the man who lifts America higher, by just so much makes higher the civilization of all mankind.

Now Mr. Choate has here in our life done the two cardinal duties of minding his own business well and also minding the business of the State. Neither will do by itself. We do not wish the aid of those excellent people who can manage the affairs of other people but not their own. (Laughter.) Nor yet of those who are content to benefit themselves but to leave the work of the State undone. The great note in the work that has been done by this Club has been the note of disinterested labor for the common good by men who have shown that they could take care of their own affairs. In the presence of Mr. Choate, in the presence of our host of the evening, of Mr. Root, I wish to pay a brief tribute on behalf of those men who have held public office, to the disinterested labor and assistance given by those men who have not held public office and who gave their labor wholly without hope of reward. You, all of you, here who have been Mr. Choate's lifelong friends, who have known him intimately, know that there has never been a movement for the betterment of America, a movement to better our State or our social life, an effort to make our politics more honest, more straightforward, more representative of the best hope and thought of the community, in which you have not been able to count upon the generous and disinterested assistance of Mr. Choate. I myself know well what I owe to Mr. Choate; and I know you will not think that I wander from our subject of this evening when I say that I appreciate to the full the way in which both Mr. Choate and Mr. Root have helped me when I have needed to draw upon all that I could draw upon in the way of intelligence and disinterested interest in the public good. It is a peculiar pleasure to see a man who has served the State so disinterestedly, with such genuine ability and without the least idea of reward in the way of office, chosen to fill one of the most honorable offices in the land, not because he has sought it (for it came to him before he had a chance to seek it), but because of the sentiment of the people that they wished at this time to be represented by one of those men who make all of us proud of being Americans. (Applause.) And we may well feel satisfied, not merely with having Mr. Choate as Ambassador, but with the political conditions which have rendered it possible, in choosing the man who should represent us to a country with which we have the closest and most intimate ties of blood and of friendship, to pay heed solely to the eminent fitness of the man himself, and to the worth of the spirit which he has so nobly represented. (Applause.)

Mr. Root: Gentlemen, may I have your attention for a moment while I read a telegram from one of the guests of the evening who had accepted our invitation ; a telegram from Philadelphia. "Train delayed renders my presence impossible. Convey to the Committee my deep regrets and to the distinguished guest my hearty felicitations. Thomas C. Platt." (Applause.)

And now I read as the closing sentiment of congratulation and felicitation to our friend, the words of a letter from the Archbishop of New York, Archbishop Corrigan, who is absent in Florida, in response to an invitation to be present: "I specially regret my absence from home at this time as it would have been a great pleasure to join with the Club in testifying respect and admiration for the gentleman whose splendid attainments have called him to represent his native country at the most distinguished Court in the world ; for whom his many friends will cordially wish that his successes in diplomacy may be as brilliant as his achievements at the Bar, and that his home-coming may be in safety, in health and in joy." (Applause.)

Now, gentlemen, I ask you to rise and to drink standing and in silence to the memory of the departed Chief Magistrate of our Sister Republic, called away untimely by Providence from the leadership of that great nation in its hour of difficulty and danger ; a Chief Magistrate who illustrated the virtues of the French people, ever true to the principles of liberty ; deplored alike by his own people and by all lovers of liberty the world over; in sympathy with the people of our sister Republic and in sad memory of Félix Faure.

The toast was drunk standing and in silence.

Mr. Root : (Turning to Mr. Choate.) And now, old friend, good-bye; *au revoir*.